NORMANDY, 75 YEARS LATER

Revisiting Normandy after D-Day

Dennis P. Klein

BOOKLOGIX·
Alpharetta, GA

ISBN: 978-1-61005-432-4

Library of Congress Control Number: 2017917381

10 9 8 7 6 5 4 3 2   0 1 1 1 2 2

♾ This paper meets the requirements of ANSI/NISO Z39.48-1992 (Permanence of Paper)

This book is dedicated to the troops that fought so gallantly on foreign soil, especially those whose lives ended abruptly during the Normandy Campaign. Also, let us never forget the French civilians who lost their lives for the freedom of their fellow countrymen.

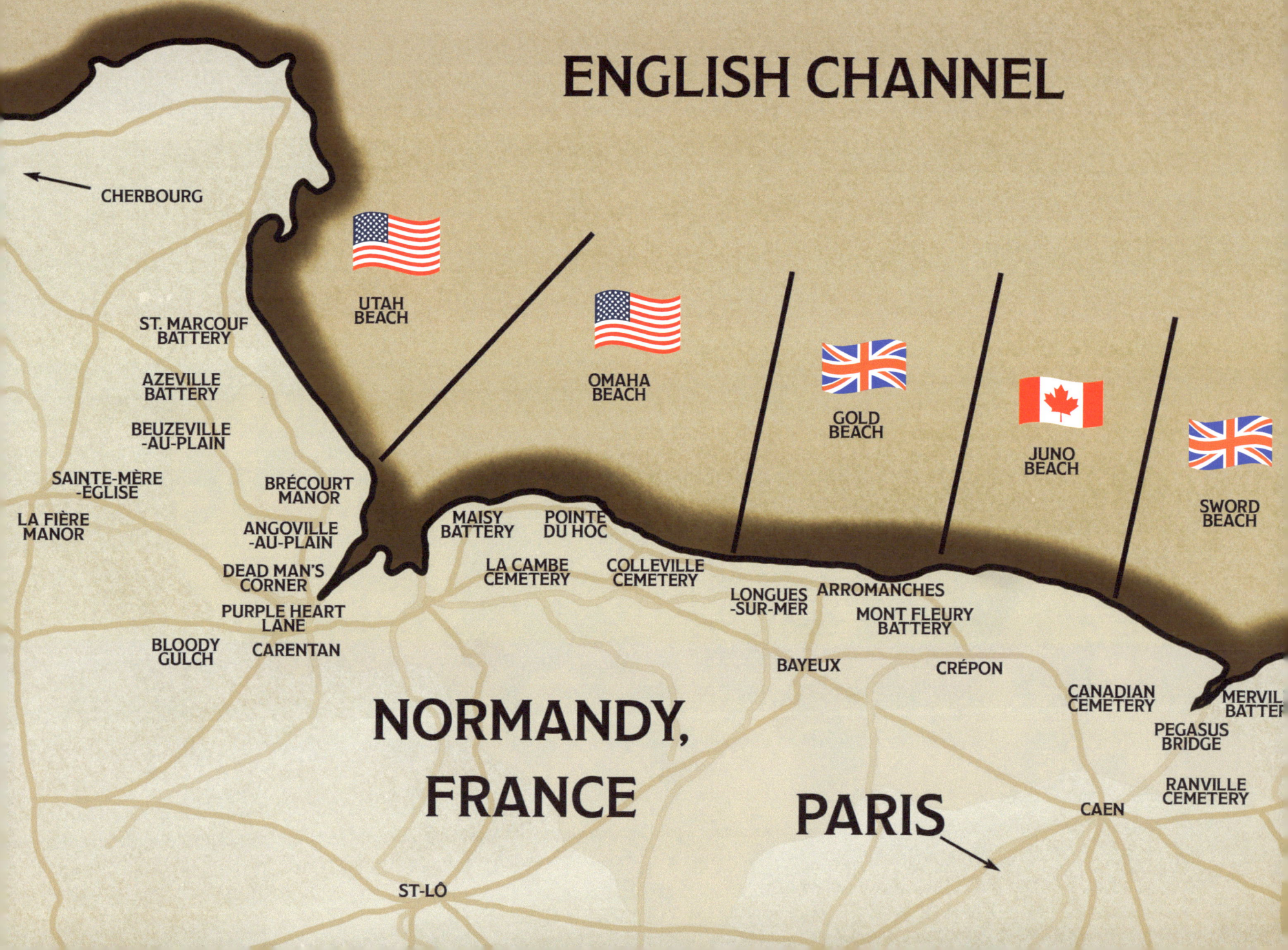

ENGLISH CHANNEL

← CHERBOURG

UTAH BEACH

ST. MARCOUF BATTERY

AZEVILLE BATTERY

BEUZEVILLE -AU-PLAIN

SAINTE-MÈRE -EGLISE

LA FIÈRE MANOR

BRÉCOURT MANOR

ANGOVILLE -AU-PLAIN

DEAD MAN'S CORNER

PURPLE HEART LANE

BLOODY GULCH

CARENTAN

MAISY BATTERY

POINTE DU HOC

LA CAMBE CEMETERY

COLLEVILLE CEMETERY

OMAHA BEACH

GOLD BEACH

JUNO BEACH

SWORD BEACH

LONGUES -SUR-MER

ARROMANCHES

MONT FLEURY BATTERY

BAYEUX

CRÉPON

CANADIAN CEMETERY

MERVIL BATTER

PEGASUS BRIDGE

RANVILLE CEMETERY

CAEN

NORMANDY, FRANCE

PARIS →

ST-LÔ

INTRODUCTION

On the northern coast of France lies Normandy, a region of seaside cliffs, sandy beaches, and winding roads connecting quaint villages and hamlets. Although Normandy is noted for its apple cider, Camembert cheese, cows, hedgerows, and stone farmhouses, the events of seventy-five years ago are what define the region today.

On June 6, 1944, everything in Normandy changed. A fifty-mile stretch of German-occupied and heavily fortified coastline, known as the Atlantic Wall, was stormed by American, British, and Canadian troops in an attempt to gain a foothold on French soil. By sunset, 156,000 combatants had arrived by parachute, glider, and boat to become the largest combined airborne-and-amphibious assault in military history. The objective of this operation was to establish a beachhead allowing additional troops to land. Following this invasion, the Nazis were driven out of France, the Netherlands, and across the Rhine River, destroying Adolf Hitler's Third Reich and ending World War II in Europe. By the end of the Normandy Campaign, 425,000 Allied and German troops were either killed, wounded, or missing.

It is said that time heals all wounds, but some scars of this historic battle remain. German bunkers and gun emplacements, now silent, are scattered throughout the grassy knolls. Bomb craters, now covered in vegetation, remain recognizable. Gravestones of fallen soldiers in cemeteries throughout the region are perpetual reminders of the lives that ended too soon.

Peace has now returned to Normandy. The blood-soaked beaches have been cleansed by the waves of the English Channel. The cows and Camembert cheese have returned. Screams and gunfire have been replaced by the sounds of wind in the bluffs above and the pounding of the surf below. The smell of apple blossoms and cider have replaced the stench of gunpowder and death. All is well in Normandy, but history will never let us forget the events that occurred here in June of 1944, the battle known as "Operation Overlord."

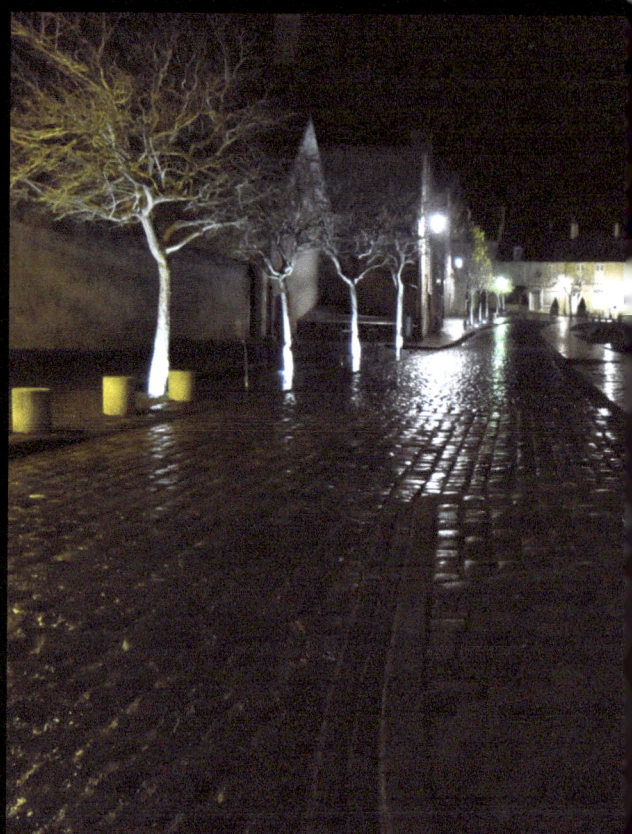

OMAHA

June 6, 1944, at 00:16, 181 men of the Ox and Bucks Light Infantry Regiment, under British Army Officer Major John Howard, landed in Horsa gliders and captured two German-held bridges. Only four hundred yards separated the Ranville Bridge over the River Orne and the Bénouville Bridge over the Caen Canal. They were later named Horsa Bridge and Pegasus Bridge, respectively, in honor of the British 6th Airborne Division. The Gondrée Café alongside the Pegasus Bridge is thought to be the first French house liberated during "Operation Overlord."

PEGASUS
BRIDGE

The British 6th Airborne Division landed near this bridge
on the night of 5th June 1944, as a spearhead to the
Allied Armies of Liberation.

La 6ème Division Aéroportée Britannique a atterri à proximité
de ce pont dans la nuit du 5 juin 1944, en tant que flèche
des Armées Alliées de Libération.

CAEN 10

Five of the six Horsa gliders landed in close proximity to the bridges, forty-seven yards from the Bénouville Bridge, while one landed seven miles off course. The mission of capturing these bridges, codenamed "Operation Deadstick," was accomplished within ten minutes of landing, signaling the start of D-Day, also known as "The Longest Day."

The British cemetery in Ranville, near Pegasus Bridge, has 2,560 soldiers interred, mostly from the 6th Airborne Division.

Lieutenant Den Brotheridge and his platoon were the first troops to reach the bridge. While releasing a hand grenade and killing a German machine gunner, Brotheridge was shot and killed at Pegasus Bridge. He is now considered to be the first Allied soldier to die in combat during the invasion.

Memorial where the Horsa glider carrying Maj. John Howard and Lt. Den Brotheridge's platoon landed near the Caen Canal.

En Reconnaissance du 1er Soldat Anglais Tombé au Pont de Benouville le 6 Juin 1944

En souvenir de la Famille GONDREE 1er Français dé...

LIEUTENANT
H.D. BROTHERIDGE
THE OXFORDSHIRE AND
BUCKINGHAMSHIRE LIGHT INF
AIRBORNE
6TH JUNE 1944 AGE 29

June 6 at 00:50, six hundred men of the 9th Parachute Battalion parachuted in to destroy the Merville Gun Battery. The drop went badly, as troops were scattered and only one hundred fifty men under British Commander Lt. Colonel Terence Otway landed close enough to assault the battery, which was protecting the village of Ouistreham and Sword Beach. When the battle ended, only seventy-five troops were able to continue on to the village of Le Plein.

Monument at C-47 crash site in Beuzeville-au-Plain. In the early hours of June 6, Plane #66, carrying five flight-crew members along with First Lieutenant Thomas Meehan III, commander of E Company 506th PIR of the 101st Airborne, and sixteen of his fellow "currahees," crashed after being hit by German flak. All aboard perished. Currahee, an Indian word for "stand alone," was the paratroopers' motto as they jumped into the darkness behind enemy lines.

Memorials dedicated to the fourteen thousand gallant soldiers from the 3rd Canadian Division who landed on Juno Beach. Underwater shoals and reefs caused havoc with the landing craft, and once ashore, they encountered heavy resistance from the Germans. Within two hours, fire support from the amphibious tanks of the 2nd Canadian Armoured Brigade were able to clear most of the coastal defenses.

The remains of a German bunker sit silently along the shore of Juno Beach.

"La Flamme" Monument, a large metal flame, sits atop a German bunker as a tribute to the twenty-nine thousand British commandos who landed at Sword Beach on D-Day.

Bill Millin, better known as "Piper Bill," was instructed to play the bagpipes by Brigadier Lord Lovat as the first wave came ashore at Sword Beach. Wearing a kilt, Bill continued playing as men fell around him during the height of the battle. He continued playing all the way to Pegasus Bridge, where he rendezvoused with Maj. John Howard.

The concrete antitank obstacles, known as "Dragon's Teeth," are still visible in the sand at Sword Beach.

The memorials in the Gold Beach sector are dedicated to the twenty-five thousand British commandos whose primary objectives were to capture Port-en-Bessin, Arromanches, and Bayeux.

In Crépon stands the Green Howards Memorial for the fallen soldiers of the British 6th and 7th Battalions. On D-Day, Sergeant Maj. Stanley Hollis attacked two pillboxes at Mont Fleury Battery, killing two German soldiers and taking the remainder as prisoners. Later that day, he destroyed an enemy field gun at Crépon. The monument features Stanley Hollis, the only recipient of the Victoria Cross awarded on D-Day.

A gun encasement at Gold Beach was strategically positioned to destroy the Allied troops as they came ashore.

Wheat field at the edge of Mont Fleury Gun Battery.

Mont Fleury Battery, located near the villages of Mont Fleury and Ver-sur-Mer, was still under construction on D-Day.

Hidden from history for sixty years, Maisy Battery was the largest German defensive position between Omaha Beach and Utah Beach, six kilometers southwest of Pointe du Hoc. Today, questions regarding the significance of this battery remain. Why was Maisy Battery not plotted on any maps prior to the invasion? Why did US Army Rangers attack an empty gun battery at Pointe du Hoc instead of concentrating on the Maisy Battery? Why was this battery, carefully buried under soil, secretively hidden after the invasion?

What events took place at Maisy Battery between June 6 and June 9, the day the guns were finally silenced? For now, the secrets remain with the empty bunkers and weapons of Les Perruques, La Martiniere, and Foucher Farm, the three batteries that formed Maisy Battery.

The Phoenix breakwaters, visible from the village of Arromanches, are concrete caissons that were towed across the English Channel to construct an artificial harbor, codenamed Mulberry B. It became known as Port Winston after Winston Churchill, the prime minister of the United Kingdom.

Steel roadways, known as "whales," floated on steel pontoons and extended one mile out into the English Channel. They were used to offload vehicles, supplies, and troops, and were an integral part of the temporary, portable, artificial harbor Mulberry B. The concrete emplacements for the German radar station remain visible on the bluff overlooking Arromanches. It had been bombed in May, prior to the invasion, and was not operating on D-Day.

The remnants of Mulberry B are visible in the sands of Arromanches. This temporary port was used to land 2.5 million men, 500,000 military vehicles, and 4 million tons of supplies for five months before it was decommissioned. Mulberry A, a similar artificial harbor at Omaha Beach, was destroyed shortly after completion by a severe storm.

Remains of Mulberry B surround the village of Arromanches.

Longues-sur-Mer Battery, situated between Omaha Beach and Gold Beach, was part of the German Atlantic Wall. It consisted of four 152 mm guns, an observation command post, and several defensive machine-gun emplacements that overlooked the Normandy coast. The battery was put out of commission during the D-Day invasion, but some of the guns still remain intact today.

The Longues-sur-Mer Battery opened fire at 06:05 hours and fired a total of 170 shots throughout the day before the guns were finally silenced.

The position of the Longues-sur-Mer Battery, several hundred yards beyond the cliffs' edge, made visual contact of the battery impossible from the channel. The guns of this battery were capable of firing thirteen miles out to sea.

(Top) A German observation post at Longues-sur-Mer sits on the edge of a cliff sixty meters above the water. Due to heavy bombing prior to the invasion, communication lines were not operating properly, making it difficult to calculate accurate firing range for the guns. (Bottom) View from inside the observation post where Allied ships were first seen.

For three days, a battle raged around the church in Angoville-au-Plain as possession changed numerous times. Two medics of the Screaming Eagles 101st Airborne, Robert Wright and Ken Moore, treated eighty wounded American and German soldiers along with a civilian French child. The church became a sanctuary, and no weapons were allowed inside.

Bloodstains on the pews of the church in Angoville-au-Plain serve as a reminder.

Memorial near Brécourt Manor where First Lt. Richard Winters of the 101st Airborne Division, along with twelve other men, parachuted into Normandy in the early hours of D-Day. They destroyed four German 105 mm howitzers, which were hidden in the tree line behind the monument.

Located between Le Grand Chemin and Sainte-Marie-du-Mont, and surrounded by pastures in hedgerow country, lies Brécourt Manor. Manned by sixty German soldiers, this battery was camouflaged by a tree line (above) and used to fire on the causeway leading off Utah Beach.

The road to Sainte-Mère-Église. Private John Steele of the 82nd Airborne was caught on the spire of this Sainte-Mère-Église church while parachuting during the early hours of June 6. He hung limply for two hours, pretending to be dead, before the Germans took him prisoner. He later escaped and rejoined the 505th Parachute Infantry Regiment.

In the early hours of June 6, approximately thirty men from the 82nd Airborne parachuted into the town square of Sainte-Mère-Église. A nearby house caught fire, possibly due to a marker flare dropped by the pathfinders. Using this water pump, a bucket brigade was formed by the townspeople to extinguish the fire. The flames from this fire illuminated the sky, making the parachutists easy targets for the German soldiers.

Views inside the church showing the pews and a stained-glass window commemorating the D-Day landings of the 82nd and 101st Airborne Divisions.

es fils ensevelissent leurs pères
en temps de guerre,
les pères ensevelissent leurs fils

In peace, sons bury their fathers,
In war, fathers bury their sons

HERODOTE

Le Merderet

« je ne connais pas de meilleur endroit pour mourir »

Lieutenant Dolan,
505e PIR
82e division aéroportée

"There's no better place to die"

Lieutenant Dolan,
505th PIR
82nd airborne division

Manoir de La Fière, west of Sainte-Mère-Église, consists of a stone bridge and a group of stone buildings. The bridge spans the Merderet River, and a five hundred–yard causeway connects the bridge to the hamlet of Cauquigny. Attacking from different fronts, Generals Matthew B. Ridgeway and James M. Gavin of the 82nd Airborne Division were able to secure the La Fière Bridge and Cauquigny. Sixty Allied soldiers were killed and another 529 were wounded or missing.

DU 6 JUIN A L'AUBE AU 9 JUIN APRES-MIDI SECTEUR DU MERDERET

FROM DAWN ON JUNE 6TH UNTIL THE AFTERNOON OF JUNE 9TH AT THE RIVER MERDERET

9 JUIN JUNE 9TH

A l'ouest de Sainte-Mère-Église, la 82e division aéroportée doit contrôler les ponts de la Fière et de Chef-du-Pont qui traversent les marais inondés par les Allemands.

- - - - - - - - - - - - - - - - -

6 Juin au petit matin

La compagnie A du 505e PIR aux ordres du lieutenant Dolan ainsi que des éléments du 507e et du 508e régiment, prennent d'assaut le manoir ainsi que le pont de la Fière. En fin d'après-midi, les Allemands appuyés par des blindés attaquent le pont. Un canon de 57 mm, récupéré dans un planeur et placé au-dessus du manoir, est détruit par le premier char. Mais quatre hommes postés près du pont avec deux bazookas détruisent les blindés allemands (l'un d'eux, Marcus Heim a laissé son nom à la route de la Fière). Dans l'attaque, le major Kellam, commandant le 1er bataillon du 505th PIR est tué.

7 Juin Les Allemands lancent une contre-attaque après une forte préparation d'artillerie. Le 505e PIR subit de lourdes pertes mais tient sa position malgré le manque d'équipements et de munitions.

8 Juin Le groupe de parachutistes en position défensive autour du pont est renforcé par des éléments du 507e PIR du capitaine Rae. Sur les 147 hommes de Dolan, seuls 81 sont encore en vie. Les attaques allemandes se poursuivent de part et d'autre du Merderet.

9 Juin Le général Gavin lance un assaut à travers les zones inondées afin de prendre et de sécuriser la chaussée. Les pertes sont effroyables dans les deux camps. Mais les hommes du 507e PIR et du 325e régiment de planeurs soutenus par des blindés arrivés de la plage d'Utah parviennent à prendre définitivement le village de Cauquigny.

La bataille de la Fière a duré trois jours, elle marque les esprits par l'intensité des combats et l'importance des pertes en hommes et en matériel pour les deux camps.

To the west of Sainte-Mère-Église, the 82nd Airborne Division must gain control of the bridges at La Fiere and Chef-du-Pont, which span the marshes that the Germans have flooded.

June 6th in the early hour of the morning "A" Company, of the 505th PIR commanded by Lt. Dolan, along with some displaced men from the 507th and 508th regiments, attack and capture the La Fiere bridge and the nearby manor house.
Later that day, German infantry and tanks, return to attack the bridge. A 57mm gun, which had arrived by glider, and set up on higher ground above the manor house is destroyed by the first tank. Four men armed with two bazookas, positioned near to the bridge, manage to knock out the German tanks. (The road to La Fiere nows bears the name of one of these men – Marcus Heim). During the battle, Major Kellam, the commanding officer of the 1st battalion of the 505th PIR is killed.

June 7th Following a sustained artillery bombardment, the Germans launch another counter attack. The 505th PIR suffers heavy losses but stands its ground, despite overwhelming odds and a severe lack of equipment and ammunition.

June 8th The group of paratroopers defending the bridge receives reinforcements from the 507th PIR commanded by Captain Rae. Of the 147 men originally assembled by Lt. Dolan, only 81 are still alive. The Germans continue to counter attack on both sides of the Merderet river.

June 9th In order to secure control of the crossing, General Gavin launches an all out assault over the flooded marshes. The casualties on both sides are horrific, but the men of the 507th PIR and the 325th Glider Infantry Regiment supported by tanks brought in from Utah Beach succeed in occupying once and for all, the village of Cauquigny on the other side.

The battle at La Fiere lasted for 3 days and has become legendary due to the ferocity of the combat and the huge losses incurred in men and equipment to both sides.

"Iron Mike" stands next to the La Fière Bridge as a tribute to the American airborne soldiers. The monument looks across the Merderet River toward Cauquigny, where the 505th Parachute Infantry and 325th Glider Regiment fought against repeated German attacks, holding the bridge for four days. Prior to the invasion, the Germans flooded the surrounding fields, turning the Merderet River into a lake with an exposed causeway between the bridge to the hamlet of Cauquigny.

The hamlet of Cauquigny, located near the once-flooded marsh at the end of the La Fière causeway, consists of six buildings, including a stone chapel. The German troops held a defensive position here for four days, five hundred yards from the La Fière Bridge, before finally retreating. (Opposite page) Bullet holes in the church are evidence of the skirmish that ensued here for control of the bridge.

PFC Charles N. DeGlopper

MEDAL
OF
HONOR

NUIT DU 8 AU 9 JUIN 1944
Le Sacrifice du Soldat de Première Classe
CHARLES N. DeGLOPPER
Cie.<<C>>, 1/325ème Régiment d'Infanterie des Planeurs
de la 82ème Division Airborne
(C Co., 1/325th Glider Infantry Regiment, 82nd AB)
<< Médaillé d'Honneur du Congrès >>

Juin 2008

Private First Class Charles N. DeGlopper of the 82nd Airborne posthumously received the Medal of Honor for his heroic actions near the La Fière causeway on June 9. Kneeling and bleeding profusely, he distracted the Germans with automatic weapon fire, allowing the remainder of his platoon to escape toward the Merderet River through a break in the hedgerow.

Crisbecq Battery, near St. Marcouf, protected the Utah Beach area, sinking the USS *Corry* and crippling several other ships during the early morning hours of D-Day. The battery was captured by the Allies on the morning of June 12.

Strong sea currents at Utah Beach caused the landings to occur 1.8 kilometers farther south than planned, placing the troops out of artillery range of the Azeville Battery. Although projectiles from this battery were capable of reaching the beach, the opening in the gun emplacements did not allow the barrels to rotate far enough to impact the landing zone.

In an attempt to camouflage the bunkers at Azeville, the Germans painted them with images of windows, stone walls, and trees. The battery was captured on June 9 by the US 22nd Infantry Regiment arriving from Utah Beach.

Utah Beach was the westernmost of the five landing beaches on D-Day. The US 4th Infantry landed 21,000 men at the beach and suffered 197 casualties. Unbeknownst to the troops, strong sea currents at Utah Beach caused the landings to occur two thousand yards farther south than planned. Soon it became apparent that the new landing site was more advantageous, being less vulnerable to the German artillery.

HIGGINS BOAT MONUMENT

On June 6, 1944 the majority of Allied troops initially arriving on the Normandy Beaches landed in one of two craft: the British Landing Craft Assault (LCA) or the American Landing Craft, Vehicle, Personnel (LCVP). In fact, some 1,089 LCVPs took part in D-Day.

Developed by Andrew Jackson Higgins in 1941, the LCVP was built by Higgins Industries in New Orleans. The Higgins Boat carried up to 36 troops, was capable of up to 12 knots and could be outfitted with a pair of Browning M1919 machine guns. The boats were crewed by four personnel.

By the time of the Normandy landings the LCVP had been used in every theatre of operations including Operation Torch in North Africa, landings in Italy, and in southern France. It was also used in the Pacific theatre.

This memorial to Higgins, his boats, and the men who rode ashore in them has been given to the people of France by the citizens of Columbus, Nebraska, the birthplace of Andrew Jackson Higgins. The memorial here is a replica of a memorial built in Columbus in 2001, and is also a celebration of partnership between Columbus and Sainte Marie du Mont ... two communities tied together by history and a heritage of freedom.

Higgins boats were developed and built by Higgins Industries in New Orleans, Louisiana. Designed for the shallow water, these plywood, flat-bottomed boats were used to transport thirty-six men at a time from ships at sea to the Normandy beaches.

The landing at Omaha Beach was scheduled for low tide to avoid German-placed obstacles in the sand. With the tide out, Omaha Beach had three hundred yards of sand to cross before reaching the shingle, a bank of small stones which measured up to eight feet high and fifty feet wide. As the tide came in, the beach became narrower, trapping men against the seawall and making Omaha Beach the bloodiest of the D-Day beaches.

OMAHA BEACH

VIERVILLE _/MER_   6 JUIN 4

SECTEUR

CHARLIE   DOG GREEN

The monument for the 29th National Guard Division sits on a German blockhouse at the Vierville Beach exit. It was here that US forces suffered the greatest number of casualties on June 6. Bedford, Virginia, a town of thirty-two hundred people, lost nineteen young men that morning, and an additional three men were lost later in the Normandy Campaign. Based on population, it was the highest casualty rate for any US town. The men became known as the "Bedford Boys."

THIS MARKS
THE SITE
OF FIRST
AMERICAN
CEMETERY
IN FRANCE
WORLD WAR II
SINCE
MOVED TO
AMERICAN
CEMETERY N°. I

Emplacement du 1er cimetière américain
Débarquement de Juin 1944

1st Infantry Division
29th Infantry Division
5th Engineer Special Brigade
6th Engineer Special Brigade

Omaha Beach D-Day Monument dedicated to the 1st and 29th Infantry Divisions.

From the edge of the American cemetery in Colleville-sur-Mer on a bluff overlooking "Bloody Omaha" Beach, only the sounds of the distant surf and lightly blowing wind can be heard today. The strip of sand is where the heaviest fighting occurred on D-Day, resulting in the highest casualties for the day.

The view from inside German bunkers overlooking Omaha Beach. The gun encasements were built into the sides of the bluffs with barrels aiming down the beach, not out to sea, allowing them to avoid a frontal bombardment from Allied ships. German General Field Marshall Erwin Rommel devised this tactic, known as enfilading fire, which placed the Allied troops inside the "kill box" once on shore.

The view of Omaha Beach at low tide, as it was when forty-three thousand Allied troops began the initial assault from the channel on D-Day. Smoke and obstacles are no longer present on the three hundred yards of golden-brown sand, and the bluffs where the enemy once hid now serve as a serene backdrop.

The monument dedicated to the 1st US Infantry Division, known as "The Big Red One," sits on a bluff above Omaha Beach on a peaceful morning. Shortly after H-hour on June 6, Col. George Taylor, commander of the 16th Infantry Regiment, told his men, "There are two kinds of people who are staying on this beach—those who are dead and those who are going to die. Now let's get the hell out of here."

To the heroic Ranger Commandoes
D2RN E2RN F2RN
of the 116th Inf
who under the command of
Colonel James E. Rudder
of the First American Division
attacked and took possession of
the Pointe du Hoc

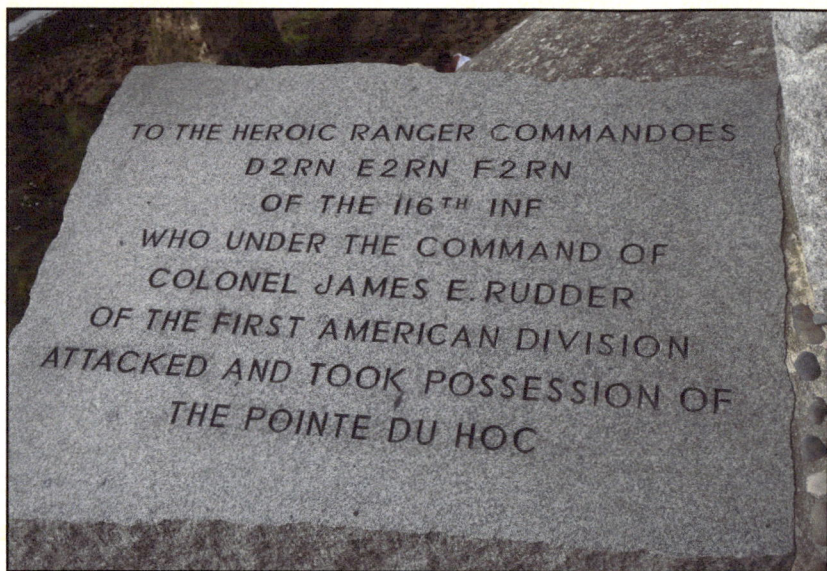

COMPETENCE | COURAGE | SACRIFICE

POINTE DU HOC

THIS SITE WITNESSED EXTRAORDINARY ACTS OF COURAGE DURING THE ALLIED INVASION OF NORMANDY.

In World War II, German forces occupied Pointe du Hoc and transformed the quiet spot into a fortified stronghold protecting a battery of heavy guns. On the morning of June 6, 1944, US Army Rangers scaled 90-foot cliffs to capture this heavily defended position and then held it against repeated counterattacks. Their heroic actions helped to establish an Allied foothold in France and begin the liberation of Europe.

Pointe du Hoc sits on the highest point between Utah Beach and Omaha Beach. On D-Day, under Col. James Earl Rudder, two hundred and twenty-five US Army Rangers scaled the ninety-foot cliffs in an attempt to destroy six gun encasements defending the beaches. Upon reaching the top, they discovered that the guns had been removed and replaced with telephone poles as decoys. On June 8, after two days of heavy combat, ninety fighting men were finally relieved by troops arriving from Omaha Beach.

At 05:50 on June 6, the naval bombardment of Pointe du Hoc began, ending just prior to 06:30, the scheduled arrival of landing crafts carrying the US Army 2nd and 5th Ranger Battalions. The cliff resembles the lunar surface, as the scars of the bomb craters remain today.

Bomb craters at Pointe du Hoc.

A small concrete bunker with a machine gun position,
known as a tobruk, lies silent among the craters.

On June 8, a group of Stuart light tanks arriving from Utah Beach joined up with the 101st Airborne Division at the crossroads between Saint-Côme-du-Mont and Carentan. As they turned south toward Carentan, a German Panzerfaust scored a direct hit on the lead tank, killing all the occupants inside. Due to heavy fighting, the badly charred body of tank commander Lt. Walter Anderson remained hanging out of the turret from the waist up for several days. This crossroad became known as "Dead Man's Corner."

The land surrounding the highway between "Dead Man's Corner" and Carentan was flooded during the Normandy invasion. On June 11, Lt. Col. Robert Cole and 250 men from the 101st Airborne crossed this causeway over four bridges spanning the Douve River. Only 132 men, using affixed bayonets and a smokescreen, were able to reach the fortified German farmhouse at the end of the causeway. Lt. Col. Cole was posthumously awarded the Medal of Honor for this action, known as "Cole's Charge," after he was killed during Operation Market Garden in the Netherlands. Today this causeway is known as "Purple Heart Lane."

On June 13, one mile southwest of Carentan, a fierce battle erupted between the German headquarters of Manoir de Donville, the church, and the railroad bridge (opposite page) near Hill 30. Dog and Fox Companies of the 101st Airborne were driven back toward Carentan, while Easy Company, commanded by First Lt. Richard Winters, was able to hold the German advancement along the railroad embankment. This allowed sixty tanks from the 2nd Armored Division to join the counterattack, forcing the Germans to withdraw. This assault, instrumental in preventing the Germans from retaking Carentan, is known as the "Battle of Bloody Gulch."

COLE'S BAYONET CHARGE MEMORIAL

VALOR

AIRBORNE

CARENTAN
JUIN 1944

CARENTAN
A SES
ENFANTS
MORTS POUR
LA FRANCE
1914 - 1918

AUX
VICTIMES DE LA GUERRE
1939 - 1945

AIRBORNE

11 JUIN 1944

C'EST D'ICI
QUE PARTIT D'UN
"CARRÉ DE CHOUX"
L'ASSAUT DÉCISIF
DU 502ème RÉGIMENT
PARACHUTISTE DE
LA 101ème AIRBORNE
BOUSCULANT LES ALLEMANDS,
IL PERMIT LA LIBÉRATION
DE CARENTAN

HANCOCK FIELD
Champ de Hancock
CPT. FRED A. HANCOCK
C-1/502 PIR • 6 JUNE 1944

As Napoleon Bonaparte had previously done, the Germans flooded the area surrounding Carentan in 1944, making it a fortified island. Controlling the village of four thousand inhabitants, where highways and a railroad converged, became a critical objective to link the Allied forces from Utah and Omaha Beach. The Battle for Carentan lasted four days, but once the German assault was neutralized, the united forces were able to launch a concerted effort to capture the seaport of Cherbourg.

Four years of occupation allowed the Germans to establish a strong defensive position, camouflaging their movement from both aerial and infantry attacks. The fields behind the beaches were framed by manmade earthen walls embedded with rows of trees and shrubs. These framed fields, extending for many miles, became open "killing zones" as the battle transitioned from the beaches to the hedgerows. The Allied troops engaged the enemy in this labyrinth of hedgerows as they began their push on land in what would become known as the "Battle of the Bocage."

On June 14, 1944, General Charles de Gaulle stepped back on native soil to deliver a speech in Bayeux, one of the first towns to be liberated, declaring it the capital of Free France. Near the entrance of Bayeux at the Rond-Point Eisenhower is a bronze statue of Dwight D. Eisenhower, a five-star general and the supreme commander of the Allied Expeditionary Forces in Europe.

The Bayeux War Cemetery is the final resting place for 4,648 fallen soldiers, the majority of whom were British.

THEIR NAME LIVETH
FOR EVERMORE

Beny-sur-Mer, the Canadian War Cemetery, is the final resting place for 2,048 soldiers. Among the graves are nine pairs of brothers and a family who suffered a triple bereavement. In the center of the cemetery stands the Cross of Sacrifice.

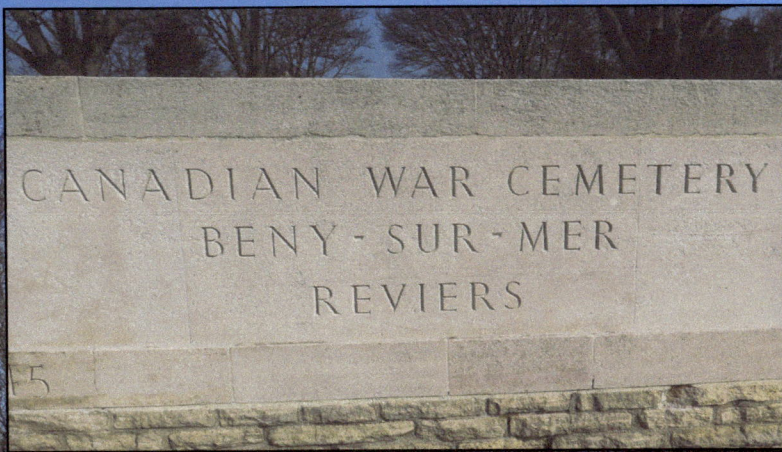

CANADIAN WAR CEMETERY
BENY - SUR - MER
REVIERS

La Cambe War Cemetery, near La Cambe, is a solemn tribute to the young German soldiers who fought so bravely along the Normandy coast. Passing from one side to the other, the narrow entrance symbolizes the lonely deaths these soldiers encountered as they were killed, one by one.

UFFZ.
ALOIS FIEDLER
*17.3.06+ 7.44

FELDW.
ERNST MÖLLER
*5.8.15+ 7.44

EIN
DEUTSCHER
+ SOLDAT +

UFFZ.
WERNER FREYER
*10.7.14+13.6.44

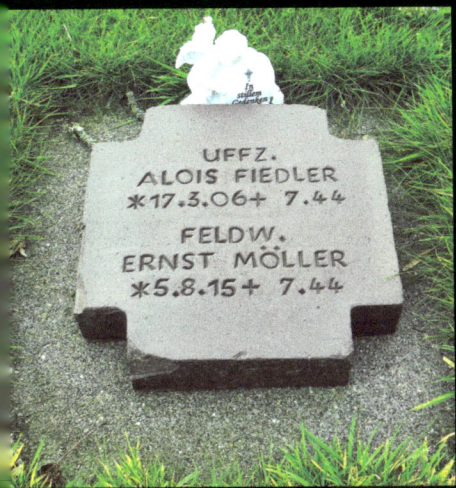

La Cambe Cemetery holds the remains of 21,222 German soldiers killed during the D-Day campaign, 80 percent of whom were under the age of twenty. Each grave holds the bodies of two German soldiers. As the Germans retreated, there was no time to care for their dead, and the task of burying the deceased fell on the Allied troops. In one grave, five German soldiers were found with five crosses stuck in the mound, hence the five stone crosses in this cemetery.

The Normandy American Cemetery and Memorial is located on a bluff above Omaha Beach near Colleville-sur-Mer. It covers 172 acres and is the burial ground for 9,387 military personnel, including four women. The 9,238 Latin crosses and 149 Stars of David are made of white Lasa marble limestone. Included are three Medal of Honor recipients and forty-five sets of brothers.

IF EVER PROOF WERE NEEDED THAT WE
FOUGHT FOR A CAUSE AND NOT FOR CONQUEST
IT COULD BE FOUND IN THESE CEMETERIES. HERE WAS
OUR ONLY CONQUEST: ALL WE ASKED... WAS ENOUGH...
SOIL IN WHICH TO BURY OUR GALLANT DEAD.

GENERAL MARK W. CLARK
CHAIRMAN, AMERICAN BATTLE MONUMENTS COMMISSION, 1969-1984

Inside the memorial at the Normandy American Cemetery is a twenty-two-foot statue symbolizing American youth rising from the waves. The Garden of the Missing contains the names of 1,557 soldiers missing in action who gave their lives in the Normandy region.

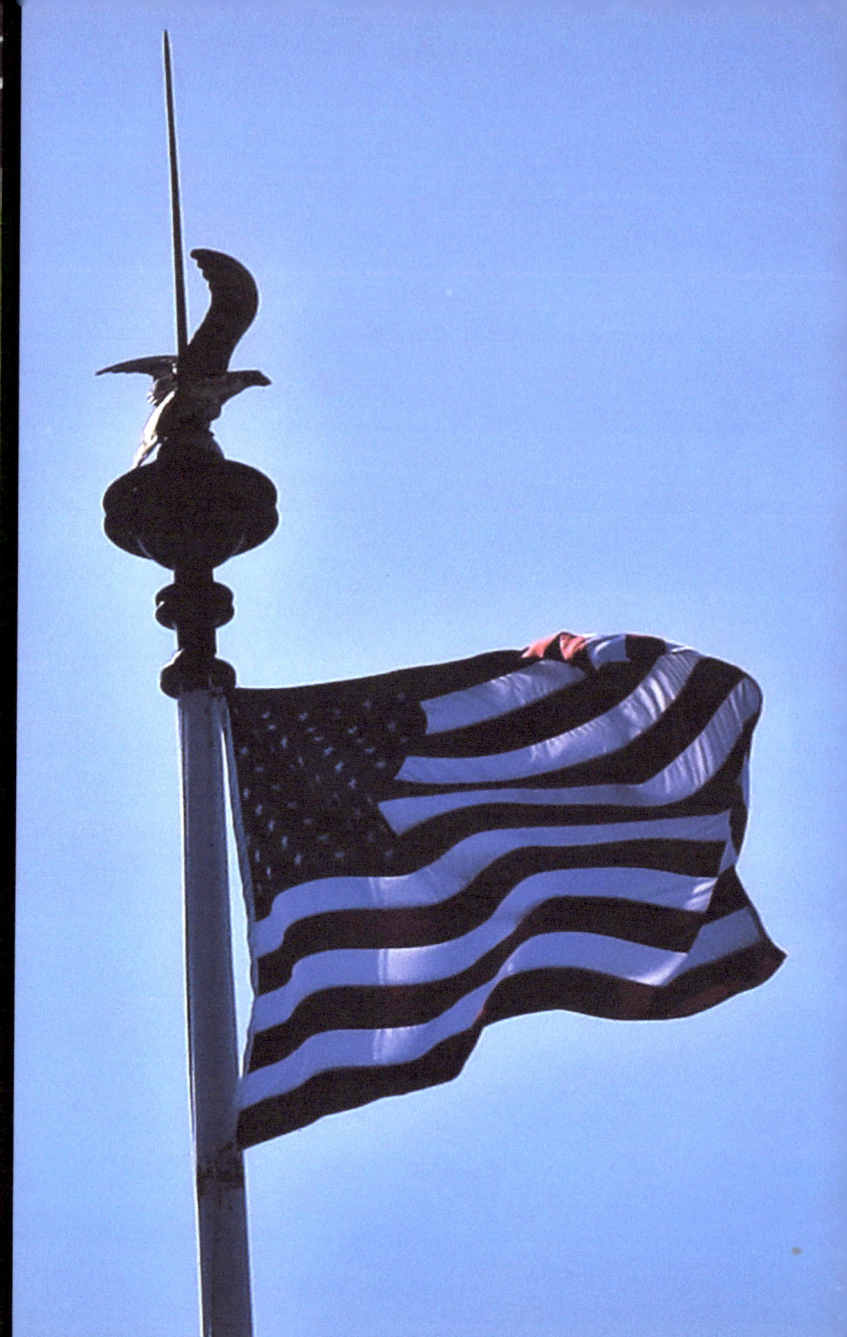

The American flag flies above the headstones of those who sacrificed their lives for it. (Lower left) A time capsule imbedded in the lawn will be opened on June 6, 2044, one hundred years after the start of "Operation Overlord."

HERE RESTS IN HONORED GLORY
A COMRADE IN ARMS
KNOWN BUT TO GOD

Aviator Quentin Roosevelt was killed in aerial combat during World War I. His body was buried in Chamery, France, but later exhumed and reburied with his brother, Theodore Jr., who died in Normandy after suffering a heart attack. Both men were sons of President Theodore Roosevelt.

View from the cemetery looking toward Omaha Beach.

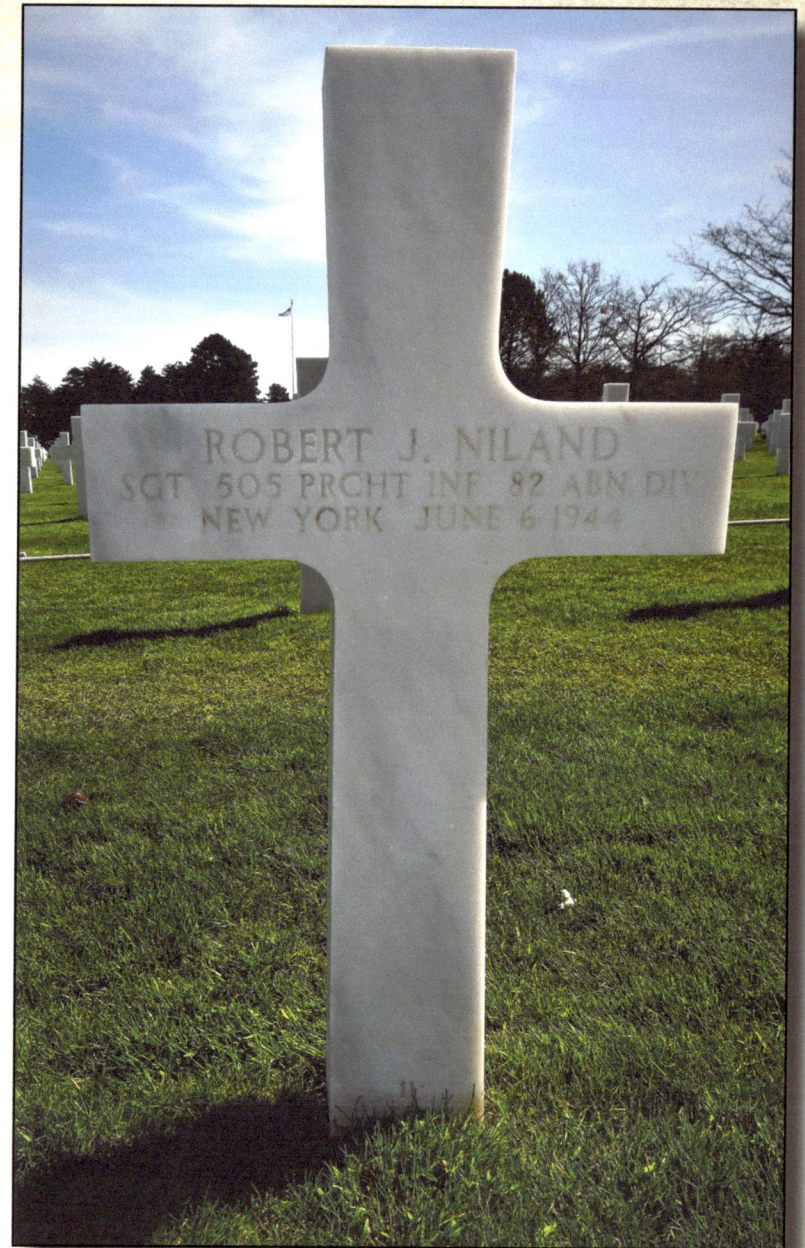

The Niland brothers, four American brothers of Irish descent, lived in Tonawanda, New York, prior to enlisting in the military. Edward was listed as missing in action and presumed dead, but was found alive as a POW after the war ended. Preston and Robert were killed near the beaches of Normandy. After the reported deaths of his three brothers, Fritz was sent back to the United States to complete his military duties.

Glancing back while leaving the cemetery, a lasting memory is made. Each headstone, standing erect and in formation, faces west, the direction of home and the United States of America.

ABOUT THE AUTHOR

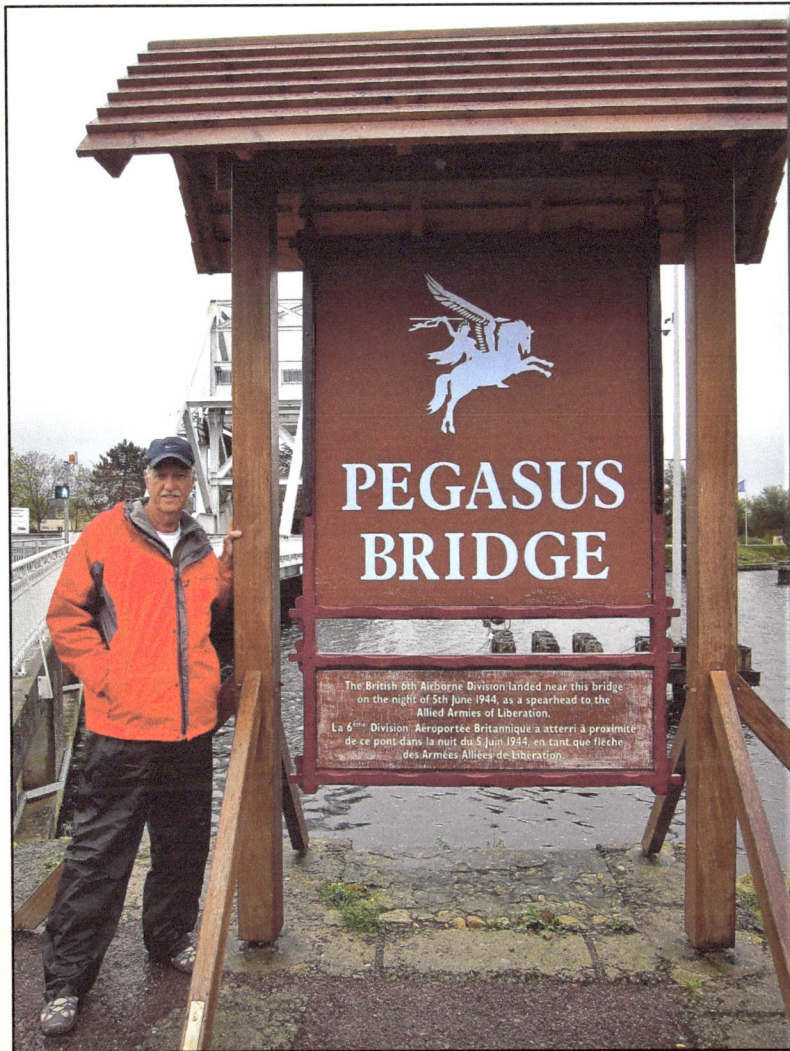

Dennis P. Klein grew up in Adams, a small town in western Massachusetts. He has spent the last twenty-five years residing in Roswell, Georgia. With a desire for aviation, Dennis graduated from East Coast Aero Technical School in Lexington, Massachusetts, and Embry Riddle Aeronautical University in Daytona Beach, Florida. His career spanned thirty-eight years as a flight instructor, a corporate pilot, and as a crew member with Eastern Airlines. He retired after flying twenty-five years with Delta Airlines. Dennis's interest in Normandy began while flying trips to Europe approaching the northern coast of France. On cloudless mornings, he often looked down and wondered what the thoughts were of those boys on that fateful morning as they embarked on their journey across the English Channel. Was it to be their finest hour?

To contact the author, please email
Normandy75years@gmail.com

www.ingramcontent.com/pod-product-compliance
Lightning Source LLC
Chambersburg PA
CBHW040710150426

42811CB00061B/1808